Making My Room Special

Emilie Barnes

with Anne Christian Buchanan

Illustrations by Michal Sparks

HARVEST HOUSE PUBLISHERS

Eugene, Oregon 97402

Making My Room Special

Copyright ©1999 Emilie Barnes and Anne Christian Buchanan
Published by Harvest House Publishers
Eugene, Oregon 97402

Mr. Gifford B. Bowne II
Indigo Gate
1 Pegasus Drive
Colts Neck, NJ 07722
(732) 577-9333

Design and Production: Garborg Design Works, Minneapolis, Minnesota

Library of Congress Cataloging-in-Publication Data
Barnes, Emilie.
    Making my room special / Emilie Barnes.
        p.   cm.
    Summary: Suggests various ways of redoing a room and keeping it organized, including decorating hints, crafts, cleanup tips, storage ideas, and room-sharing solutions.
    ISBN 0-7369-0044-6
    1. Handicraft—Juvenile literature. 2. Children's rooms—Juvenile literature. 3. Interior decoration—Juvenile literature.
4. Orderliness—Juvenile literature. [1. Interior decoration. 2. Bedrooms. 3. Handicraft. 4. Orderliness.] I. Title.
TT160.B328   1999
747.7'7—dc 21
                                                  98-38010
                                     CIP
                                     AC

Printed in the United States of America.

99 00 01 02 03 04 05 06 07 08 / IP / 10 9 8 7 6 5 4 3 2 1

Contents

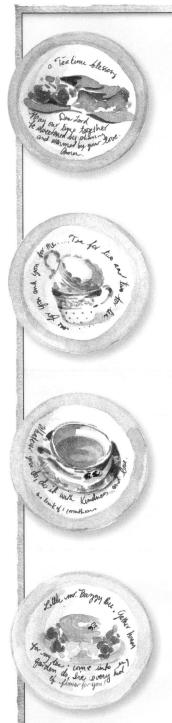

How We Started Our Room Makeover Service

Hi! I'm Emilie Marie, and I want to tell you about something great my friends and I have been doing. We've started a room makeover service!

Can you believe it? Nine years old, and we're already in business—except we're not doing it to make money. We're working together to help each other clean up and decorate our rooms. It's been so much fun that I'm thinking about doing this kind of thing when I grow up!

It didn't start out fun, though. It started with a big, sad frown on the face of my friend Elizabeth. I'd gone over to her house to see if she could go skating.

"I can't go anywhere, Emilie Marie," she said, shaking her head sadly. "I don't think I'm ever going anywhere again."

I was confused.

"It's my room," Elizabeth explained. "Mom says I can't go out of the house or have any friends over to play until I've completely cleaned it up."

Her frown got bigger, and now I knew why. I've seen Elizabeth's room!

Elizabeth, you see, is really smart. She's always willing to help someone who is having trouble with math problems or spelling words. And she's fun and creative, full of great ideas for projects that our special club, the Angels, can do. She's a really good friend!

But Elizabeth does have this one little problem—her messy room. Clothes on the floor. School papers piled up on her desk. Books and toys and everything else scattered wherever she'd finished with them. Her mother was always nagging her to clean her room, but that room never seemed to get any better.

Elizabeth was right. If she couldn't leave the house until her room was clean—maybe she'd never leave the house at all!

The door closed between me and my friend's sad face. I was standing there on the porch, skates in hand, when all of a sudden a terrific idea popped into my head.

I went straight over to my friend Christine's house to talk about it. Christine is a very good

listener, and as usual she was all ears when I told her I had an idea.

"This could be a really great Angel project," I said. "We could all work together to help Elizabeth get her room fixed up. That way it wouldn't seem like such a big job, and we could *all* go skating afterward."

"That's a great idea, Emilie Marie! You're really good at cleaning your room up fast. It takes me forever."

"But that's the thing about doing it together. It's a lot faster than doing it alone. And it's more fun, too."

"We could do it this Saturday!" Christine said. I could see she was already getting excited about the project.

"Let's call Aleesha and Maria right now," I said. (Maria and Aleesha are the other two Angels in our club.) "We need to have an Angels meeting right away. We've got to make plans!"

And that's how our room makeover service started. Sounds like fun, doesn't it? Well, you're very welcome to come join us! After all, we might have some ideas for your room, too. Oh, and remember, our first stop is Elizabeth's house!

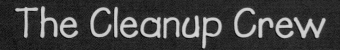

The Cleanup Crew

HOW ELIZABETH'S ROOM WENT FROM CLUTTERED TO CUTE

Pleasant sights and good reports give happiness and health.

The Book of Proverbs

Early Saturday morning, the Angels showed up at Elizabeth's house.

"I hope you brought a dump truck," joked Elizabeth's mom.

"Sorry," I laughed. "But we did bring my mom's ostrich feather duster. It's good for dust bunnies—and it makes a great turkey tail!" I held it behind me like a bunch of tail feathers, and we laughed.

"I want to get this done fast so we can go skating!" said Aleesha as we walked down the hall to Elizabeth's room.

"This'll help," said Christine. She slipped a reggae CD into Elizabeth's boom box. "We always play this at home when we clean house. It makes you want to *move*."

Christine was right. Soon we were really moving!

Flip-flop! Dirty sheets came off the bed, and on went clean ones. With a matching bed-spread pulled smooth and pillows plumped, the bed looked cozy and pretty. Elizabeth's room looked a ton better already!

Whoosh! We ran all around the room, putting things away. Maria piled dirty clothes into the hamper. Aleesha lined books up on the shelves. Christine and I stacked school papers neatly on a shelf beside the desk. Elizabeth put away her riding equipment (she *loves* horses) and

her
skates...and a surprise hiding under
the bed—her pet rabbit, Hazel.

"Uh-oh," she said. "Guess I forgot to put her
back in her cage!"

"Hope this isn't your homework!" said Aleesha
with a grin, holding up a wad of chewed-up paper.

Bit by bit, we were getting there. "There's too
many clothes in this drawer!" Maria groaned as she
tried to stuff in another T-shirt.

"Maybe I need to put away my summer
clothes," said Elizabeth.

"Not today!" I said. "Today we clean. You can
get it all organized another day."

We kept on cleaning, dancing to the music as
we went. Sometimes we laughed and acted silly.
Sometimes we just worked hard. When everything
was put away, each Angel grabbed a cleaning tool
and worked her way around the room. While we
dusted and scrubbed and vacuumed,
Elizabeth scurried around the house, deliver-
ing dirty clothes to the utility room, hair clips
to the bathroom, and dirty dishes to the kitchen.

Finally Christine called out, "All done!" We
plopped down in the middle of the floor, laughing
and giving each other hugs and high fives.

"I can't believe it!" Elizabeth said as she looked
around her nice, neat room. "Guess we got rid of all

those dust bunnies!" said Maria.

"From now on," said Elizabeth, "the only bunny
allowed in here is Hazel!"

Emilie Marie's Speedy Cleanup Steps

Use these steps when your room
hasn't been cleaned in awhile—like
Elizabeth's! The point is to get everything tidied up as fast as possible. Get
moving and get the job done!

Step One: Get it all together. Any job goes quicker
when you have a plan and everything you need
close at hand.

When we picked
up Elizabeth's room, we used...
• laundry bag for dirty clothes
• basket for things that went outside the
  room (books from living room, plates from kitchen)
• large plastic garbage bag

- feather duster (old socks work too) and yardstick for cobwebs
- all-purpose cleaner in spray bottle and cleaning cloths to wipe away dirt and gunk
- spray bottle of rubbing alcohol and a squeegee—isn't that a great word?—for windows and mirrors (or window spray and paper towels)
- vacuum cleaner, broom, or dust mop to clean the floor

Step Two: Make your bed. Strip all the dirty sheets off your bed, put on fresh ones, and your room will look better already!

Step Three: Quickly pick up three kinds of things. In most rooms, two or three kinds of things make up most of the mess. (In Elizabeth's room, we found lots of dirty clothes, school papers, and books scattered everywhere.) So make a quick run around your room and take care of the three things that are making up most of the mess. When you're finished, take a look around. With the bed made and the

biggest problems solved, doesn't it look a lot neater already?

Step Four: Pick up everything else and pile it on the bed. Look under the bed, behind furniture, on the closet floor. Anything that's out of place goes on your bed. Then put everything on the bed where it belongs— trash in the garbage bag, clothes in the closet, games on shelves. If something belongs in another room, put it in a basket for later delivery.

Step Five: When the bed is empty again, get things clean. Start right beside your door and work your way around the room, carrying a bucket of cleaning supplies and your trash bag with you. Dust off the tops of dressers, tables, and bookshelves. Use spray cleaner to get marks off the walls, fingerprints off the doors, crayon marks off your

8

desk, and to get rid of any mystery gunk you find. If windows and mirrors have fingerprints or dirt on the inside, spray them with alcohol or window cleaner. Then, working from the top down, make them sparkle and shine with a squeegee or paper towels. Once you've cleaned your way all around the room, go around it again with a vacuum or dust mop. Be sure to chase the dust bunnies out from under the furniture!

Step Six: Finish it up. When you're done cleaning, it's time to play delivery girl. Put away the cleaning supplies. Deliver the dirty laundry to the utility room. Take your basket of "outside stuff" around the house and put everything back where it belongs. Put the garbage bag in the trash. Then go back to your room and look around. Straighten the pictures. Fluff up the pillows on the bed, and put your favorite stuffed toy on top. Line up the dolls in your collection. For a special touch, pick some little flowers like pansies or violets and put them in a tiny vase. Then smile, because you're well on your way to making your room really special!

bright clothes

white clothes

dark clothes

How-To Hints
How to Make
Cleanup Fast and Fun

- Do it with a friend! Put on lively music and dance your way through.
- Make up cleaning games. Challenge yourself to vacuum the whole rug without stepping on a part you've already vacuumed. Or set a timer and race yourself.
- Imagine yourself doing something you really like—playing soccer or making bead jewelry. Remember that the sooner you finish cleaning your room, the sooner you'll get to do something fun!
- Give yourself little rewards along the way. When you've made your bed, have a chocolate chip cookie. When you've put everything away, enjoy a glass of fresh orange juice. When you're all done, go for a bike ride with a friend.

How-To Hints
How to Make a Bed
You Want to Lie In

What's the first thing you notice when you walk into a bedroom? The bed! If your bed looks cozy and neat, your whole room looks nicer. Here's how to make a great bed from the bottom up!

- **Start at the bottom.** The bottom sheet is the one with the elastic corners. Lift up the edges of the mattress and slip the corners of the sheet over the mattress corners. The last corner's the hardest!

- **Add your top sheet.** Place the top sheet on the bed "wrong" side up—with the pretty side facing the bed. The wide hem goes at the head and the narrow hem hangs off the foot of the bed. Tug and pull until the sheet is smooth and even on both sides.

- **Add a blanket.** Lay your blanket on top of the sheet with its top about eight inches from the edge of the mattress—that's about the length of this book. The bottom of the blanket will hang off the foot of the bed.

- **Tuck it tight.** This is how you make sure everything stays neat and comfortable! Fold the top edge of the sheet back over the top edge of the blanket so that the pretty side shows. Go to the foot of the bed and tuck the sheets and blankets under the mattress. If you want to, you can tuck in the sheets and blankets on the sides, too.

- **Add the finishing touches.** Put your bedspread, quilt, or comforter on top. Straighten it so it hangs down evenly on the sides and bottom. Put pillows in their shams and lay them on top of the bed or under the spread. Make sure everything looks smooth and nice. Then add little pillows and a few stuffed animals to decorate. What a comfy bed!

Things to Make Your Room Special

A PILE OF PILLOWS

You don't have to know how to sew to make some cute pillows. All you need are some throw pillows, cute fabrics, and your imagination!

> throw pillows in different shapes and sizes—
> squares, rounds, or bolsters
> something to cover the pillows—pillowcases,
> scarves, bandannas, dishtowels, cloth napkins,
> fabric remnants, even old T-shirts
> ribbons, yarn, and trim
> rubber bands
> safety pins
> scissors
> washable fabric glue

EASY SCARF PILLOW

You'll need two square scarves, bandannas, or square napkins that are eight to ten inches larger than your pillow. Lay one scarf wrong side up on a flat surface. Lay the pillow on top and cover it with the second scarf, right side up. Tie the corners together or wrap rubber bands tightly around the corners. Cover the rubber bands with pretty ribbons.

You can hold the scarves in place with safety pins that are hidden behind the ribbons or the knots.

For a comfy variation, try making the pillow with two squares of polar fleece.

CANDY-WRAP PILLOW

Find a standard or king-sized pillowcase in a color or pattern that you like. Slip a square or bolster-shaped pillow inside the case and center it so that you have an even amount of extra fabric at each side. (You can wrap any extra fabric above or below the pillow around the back.) Now catch the extra fabric tightly at each side with a rubber band and cover the bands with ribbon. This is really fun to do with holiday colors and fabrics to decorate your room for Christmas!

FACE LIFTERS

This is the easiest way to put a smile on a worn old pillow nobody uses anymore. Just use fabric glue to attach a pretty dishtowel or napkin to the front of the pillow. Another neat thing to do is to glue a crocheted doily onto a solid-color pillow for a pretty, old-fashioned look.

T-SHIRT PILLOW

It's easy to turn a T-shirt you've outgrown into a unique pillow cover. First, turn the T-shirt inside out and wrap a rubber band around each sleeve. Wrap rubber bands around the two bottom corners, too. Pin a row of safety pins just under the collar. Now carefully turn the T-shirt right-side out and slip a pillow inside it. Tuck the bottom edges under and, if you need to, close it with more safety pins. Now you can still use your favorite T-shirt—only as a fun, smushy pillow!

A Place for Everything

HOW WE HELPED MARIA SORT HER STUFF

Practice tenderhearted mercy
and kindness to others.

The Book of Colossians

"My turn next!" said Maria when the Angels met on Wednesday at my Grammie's house.

"Your turn for what?" I said.

"To get a room makeover!"

"But your room always looks great," Christine said. "It's usually pretty neat. And I like all your dolls...and your paper flowers."

"Yeah, I like it all too," said Maria. "But half the time I can't find anything! My toy box is stuffed, and my drawers are really full, and I have all these school papers, even from way back in kindergarten. And my closet—well, I'm almost afraid to open it!"

"I know what you mean," said Elizabeth, and we nodded. After all, we'd just finished cramming all of Elizabeth's stuff into drawers and closets.

"What I want to do," Maria went on, "is get it all organized. And I've got some ideas, but it'd be nice if you guys could help."

Well, we'd had so much fun getting Elizabeth's room in shape that we agreed right away. We showed up at Maria's bright and early on Saturday morning, and her dad met us at the door. "I've made something for you girls," he said. We sniffed the air and grinned. Maria's dad is a baker, and he'd made cinnamon rolls!

When we went into Maria's room, we had another surprise. It was full of empty boxes—shoe boxes, grocery boxes, even cardboard file boxes from the office store. In the middle of the room were three big plastic garbage bags, labeled THROW AWAY, GIVE AWAY, and PUT AWAY. Maria had also filled a cardboard box with school papers—old worksheets, artwork, special projects. Over in the corner were a bunch of art supplies—wrapping paper, cloth, glue, the works. And stacked in a corner were a whole

bunch of clay flower-
pots in all sizes.

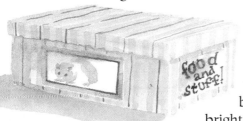

"I've
already gotten
started," said
Maria. "I've been going through my stuff and putting
it into these bags. When I've got it all sorted, I want
to get it organized in the boxes. I thought we could
cover the boxes to make them look pretty."

Soon we were hard at work. Aleesha and I
helped Maria sort through her things, deciding what
to keep and what to give away or throw away.
Meanwhile, Christine and Elizabeth got going cover-
ing the boxes with Maria's pretty
paper.

"This is
fun," said
Elizabeth as
she covered a
big shoebox in
bright, striped fabric.

"You could put hamster
stuff in here," she added, looking over at Maria's
pets running through their plastic tunnels.

Doing Maria's room took awhile, but when we
were finished, we had a much neater, much cuter
room. Boxes covered with bright paper and fabric
were stacked neatly on the shelves and tucked in

corners. Art supplies were organized into a row of
clay flowerpots. Even the hamsters' area was neat
and organized—thanks to Elizabeth's great box.

Maria's dad gave us extra cinnamon rolls on our
way out, and Maria thanked us over and over. "I
think I can finally open up my closet without being
afraid of it!" she grinned.

Put away   Give away   throw away

Trash bags

Maria's Super Sort-and-Store Plan

The point of getting organized like Maria did is to make all your stuff easy to find and to keep it from getting messed up.

Step One: Get ready to organize. The easiest way to sort your stuff is to use three big plastic garbage bags or boxes. Label one THROW AWAY, another PUT AWAY, and another GIVE AWAY. Also, if you have lots of loose papers, you might want to have another box just for them.

Step Two: Sort it out piece by piece. Start with one drawer, one shelf in your closet, or one part of your room (under the bed, the top of your desk). Pick up each item from that one area and decide where it

should go. If you want to keep it where you got it, put it back. If you want to keep it and it belongs somewhere else in your room, put it in its proper place. If you want to keep it but don't know where yet, put it aside either in the PUT AWAY bag or in the paper box. If you don't want it and nobody else could use it, put it in the THROW AWAY bag. If you don't want it but you think somebody else might, put it in the GIVE AWAY bag. When you've completely finished going through the stuff in one area, start on the area right next to it. Continue until you've worked your way around the whole room.

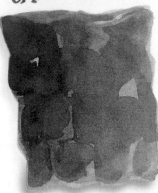

Step Three: Start thinking about new homes for your stuff. While you're sorting through everything, start to think about what goes together, how you use your stuff, and what should go where. For example, alike things should be stored together—paper with paper, doll clothes with doll clothes. Things you use together should live together. If you use pencils, brushes, and sponges for art projects, store them in the same place. Things you use often—pens, pencils, rulers, in-season clothes—should be easy to find and reach. Things you don't use often should be clearly labeled so you can remember where they are. Use boxes, crates, bins, shelves—anything that will help you organize and store your stuff. You can even cover boxes with fabric or shelves with pretty paper to help your room get organized *and* decorated!

Step Four: Put it all away. You've done the sorting and the thinking and the getting ready. Now it's time to store your "put away" stuff in its new home. Go through your bags or boxes and neatly put everything away. If you want to, make a list of where every-thing is stored. You can even number your boxes and make index cards showing what's in each one. Then it's easy to flip through your index cards to find the missing item. *My rock collection? That's in box number five, under my bed!*

Step Five: Promise yourself. Your room will stay neat and organized and easy to live in if you promise yourself to find a home for every new thing you bring into your room. Don't just toss it down on the bed. Think—*where should it live?* Then put it there right away!

How-To Hints
A Home for Everything

With a little creativity, it's not hard to find a happy home for everything in your room!

School and art supplies (pencils, pens, rulers, and scissors)
• Cut paper towel tubes into different lengths and paint them. Glue together in a cluster, then glue cluster to a cardboard base.
• Old coffee mugs make great pen and pencil holders.
• Buy some inexpensive terra cotta flowerpots like Maria did and use them to organize your supplies. Leave them plain or paint to match your room.

Artwork/schoolwork/paperwork
• Use a real metal file cabinet or a file box with colored file folders. Label folders for homework, artwork, pictures, letters and cards, whatever you want to store.
• Hang a piece of string across one wall to display

your favorite creations. Attach the art with clothespins. You can change your gallery whenever you want to!

- Old backpacks—one for each year of school—are a good way to store papers you want to keep. Small items could go in an old lunchbox.

Books and magazines

- Make a bookcase by stacking boards on bricks or cement blocks.
- A line of plastic crates makes a great bookcase.
- Store books and magazines you're reading right now in a pretty basket by your bed.

Little stuff (like beads, small toys, or dress-up jewelry)

- Checks come in small, neat boxes that are great for holding little stuff—they also make good drawer dividers.
- Divided plastic boxes from hobby stores are great for organizing beads, small shells, yarn for friendship bracelets, paper clips—almost anything!
- Baby food jars are great stuff holders. Wash them out well and soak in water until the labels come off. Then you can decorate them with acrylic paint. Or, with your parents' help, you can nail the *lids* of several baby food jars to the bottom of a shelf. Your little storage jars will hang from the shelves, and you'll have more storage in less space.

Things to Make Your Room Special

"Got You Covered" Boxes

Here's how you can cover any rectangular box, with or without a lid, with either paper or fabric.

> *box in any size, with or without lid*
> *pretty material to cover the box—fabric, wallpaper, wrapping paper, brown paper (good for stamp art!), or contact paper*
> *glue stick or tacky craft glue*
> *scissors*
> *index cards and markers*

1. Lay the bottom of the box on the wrong side of the fabric or paper. To know how much fabric or paper to use, think of wrapping a present—only without a top. Instead of the paper or fabric wrapping all around the box, it falls into and over the box's top edges (see diagram 1). Cut the fabric or paper to fit your box.

2. Using a glue stick, put glue on the outside of the box and inside the top edges where the fabric or paper will be.

3. "Wrap" fabric or paper around box, starting on one side. When the fabric or paper covers the end of the box, it naturally folds into a triangle (diagrams 2 and 2a). Glue down all areas where the fabric or paper is touching the box.

4. Repeat the process for the other side (diagram 3).

5. On the ends, glue the fabric or paper to itself in the triangle (diagram 4).

6. Put glue on the top of the triangle (diagram 5) and press it up to the end of the box (diagram 6).

7. Do the lid of the box the exact same way. Just think of it as a very shallow box!

8. Decorate your box any way you like. You can add paper cutouts, stickers, buttons, or silk flowers to the box. Use index cards and markers to make labels so you'll always know what's inside your box.

2.a

4.

glue

5.

glue

6.

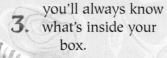

3.

A Bed of Roses

HOW WE MADE CHRISTINE'S ROOM FIT FOR A PRINCESS

The room of her dream seemed changed into fairyland—and it was flooded with warm light, for a bright lamp stood on the table covered with a rosy shade.

—Frances Hodgson Burnett
A Little Princess

"I know what I want to do for my room makeover!" Christine said one afternoon as we were walking home from school. "I want a room you'd find in a castle—a princess room."

"But your room doesn't need a makeover!" I protested. Christine's room always looked just perfect to me, like a room you'd see in a magazine. She had the cutest pink, purple, and blue sheets and really pretty wallpaper with roses all over it. And her bed was the four-poster kind, which I just love. Christine even put big pink, purple, and blue bows on her cocker spaniel, Mickey, so he'd match her room!

"Well," Christine said, "like my mom says, there's always room for improvement! And she said she'd help us make some neat stuff to redecorate."

I liked that thought. Christine's mom always has the best suggestions. All the other Angels liked the idea, too. We hurried over to Christine's house on the following Saturday to see how to decorate a room fit for a princess.

Sitting on Christine's bed was a big basket of silk roses and a pile of floaty, gauzy material. Christine said it was called *tulle* (pronounced "tool") and that people use it to make veils for brides. She and her mom had also found some lace tablecloths at a garage sale, some old-fashioned looking dishcloths with roses on them, a couple of scarves, a stack of pink and lavender sheets, and even a soft, pastel baby quilt.

"Now," said Christine, "I want you all to close your eyes and imagine a room for a princess—'cause that's what I want my room to look like."

We did! And we turned Christine's room into a castle that day by using the tulle and the roses and the ribbon to decorate everything.

First we took that floaty, gauzy fabric and wrapped it around the bedposts. We even draped it from bedpost to bedpost to make it look a little like a

make a delicate, curtain-like thing. Next we used thin wire, pipe cleaners, pins, and glue to attach those pretty silk roses to *everything*—the tulle on the bedpost, the curtains, the lampshade and wastebasket, and even on some of Christine's stuffed animals! We also covered boxes with some of the pink and lavender sheets and glued roses on top. We even put those roses around a photo frame for her bedside table.

dreamy canopy. Then we took down the curtains from her windows (leaving the window shades) and wrapped more tulle around the curtain rod, letting the ends trail down to

"Well, what do you think?" I asked Aleesha. "Is it beginning to look like a princess's room in here?"

"Looks kind of like a gardener's room to me," she said.

"Hey," said Christine, "that's a really good idea! Maybe we could redecorate with a garden theme...."

"Whoa, girl!" said Aleesha. "One room makeover at a time, please! So what do we do next?"

"Well, I think it would be fun to make a bulletin board," said Christine.

That's just what we did! And guess what we attached to her bulletin board along with pictures and postcards? You got it—more silk roses! We looked around the room, congratulating each other on a job well done. And then we crowned Christine Queen of the Roses!

Christine's Really Fabulous Decorating Tips

Tip One: Decorate your room so it looks like *you*. Choose colors that you like and that make you feel good, and display your interests and hobbies all around the room. After all, your bedroom is where you live! Do you love skating, animals, reading, sports, art? Are you the type who cozies up with the latest Nancy Drew and a cup of hot cocoa, or do you practically live in your rollerblades? People should be able to walk into your room and see you in it! Christine loves flowers and roses. Elizabeth is a big horse fan. And I (Emilie Marie) collect teacups. So guess what's in our rooms? Yep—roses, horses, and teacups!

Tip Two: Pick a theme. It's fun to choose a theme—like roses or horses—that you repeat many places in your room. It helps your room look like everything fits together, and it's a great way to show what you like to do. If you like to write to pen pals in other countries, why not fill your room with flags, maps, and posters from a travel agency? If you're an animal lover, you can decorate with a cat or dog or horse theme. If you're a sports fanatic or beach bum, your pictures and creative decorations can say that. A room with a Western theme could have a lamp made out of a boot with a bandanna shade, a lariat hung on the wall, a saddle in the corner—even a sheriff's star pinned on your favorite teddy bear. I even heard of a Hawaii room that had surfboards instead of bookshelves and a grass skirt on the bed instead of a dust ruffle. You can really use your imagination!

Tip Three: Everything doesn't have to match. Your bed and your dresser and your nightstand don't have to look exactly alike. In fact, it's much better (and more creative) to mix and match the stuff in your room.

calm you down. Sunny yellow makes most people feel happy. Earth colors can really make you feel relaxed.

Tip Five: Ask for help. Decorating is lots more fun when you do it with someone else, and it helps to have other people's opinions, too. Your mom or dad or grandparent can give you some great ideas *and* hands-on help. After all, you'll need their permission before you paint or make any big changes. And they make good decorating assistants when you're ready to paint, hang things on the walls, make crafts, or just buy what you need. Look through books and magazines to get more creative ideas. Find decorating books in your local library, or flip through some of your parents' magazines. You can also use a pad of sketch paper and some crayons or colored pencils to create your own room plan! Finally, your friends can be a lot of help when you decorate—as we found out when we started redoing our rooms. It's fun to share the ideas, and the project goes a lot faster with many hands. Why not start a room makeover club of your own?

Tip Four: Use your favorite colors. The easiest way to make even a room with mismatched furniture look like it goes together is to use your favorite colors. You can even mix up different patterns of fabric (like plaids with florals) if most of the colors are pretty much the same. Usually what works best is to choose one main color (like light green) and one or two other colors (maybe buttery yellow and periwinkle blue) that you use several places in your room. Think of what you like—bright crayon colors, ice-cream pastels, or nature-colored greens and browns. Also, did you know that the colors in your room can really change the way you feel? Reds and oranges make you feel excited. Blues and greens

How-To Hints
Little Touches that Mean a Lot

Just a few simple decorating touches can make a big difference in anyone's room. Best of all, these don't take very much time or great talent.

- Use a gold paint pen to decorate a plain lamp and its matching shade.

- Hang an inexpensive mirror and use "slick" paint to create a design around the edges of the glass.
- Decorate an old basket by weaving thin ribbon in and out among the reeds. Tie on a matching bow.
- Fancy up plain metal bookends by painting or gluing together paper or felt slip-covers. Bricks make cute book-ends, too, and can be decorated easily with spray paint. (Use a paint-brush to get rid of dust before you paint them.)
- For the easiest, quickest decorating of all, just tie big bows around the necks of all your stuffed toys!

How-To Hints
Decking the Walls

Use your imagination to find super cool and creative wall decorations. (You might need an adult to help hang some of these.)

- a colorful kite
- terra-cotta wall plaques from a garden store—like suns and moons
- a nature collage—leaves, shells, and twigs glued into a unique design on foam-core board
- a quilt or tapestry
- your very own masterpiece painted on a stretched canvas (find at a hobby store) with acrylic paints
- a big fishnet with pictures and postcards and shells caught in it

Things to Make Your Room Special

Fit-for-a-Princess Bulletin Board

This pretty bulletin board doesn't require any push-pins; just tuck your pictures, prizes, and other treasures under the ribbons. You can make it in colors to match your room!

24" by 18" piece of foam-core board from a hobby shop
26" by 20" piece of fabric ironed smooth
tacky craft glue
package of thumbtacks
about 5 feet of 1/2" ribbon in color to go with your fabric
scissors and a ruler or yardstick
decorations (buttons, bows, more ribbon, lace, silk flowers, paper cutouts)
picture frame to fit foam-core board (if you want)
thick piece of polyester batting (if you want)

1. Place the fabric wrong side up on a flat surface and lay the foam-core board in the middle. The same amount of cloth should be sticking out all around.

2. Start gluing on one of the short sides. Put a line of glue along the back of the board near this edge, but stop before you get to the corners. Wrap the extra fabric on that side around to the back and press it into the glue. Push in several thumbtacks to hold down the fabric while the glue dries. Do the same thing with the other short side and both of the long sides. Make sure the fabric is pulled smooth across the front of the

foam-core board. Glue the corners last. You'll probably have to fold or bunch the fabric before you glue it down. If it's really bulky, you can cut away some of the extra before you glue.

3. Let glue dry, then turn the board over. The pretty, covered side should be facing you. Cut a piece of ribbon long enough to go from one top corner to the opposite bottom corner, plus two inches. Cut another piece of ribbon the same length. Lay these two ribbons from corner to corner in an "X" shape, leaving about an inch of ribbon hanging off each corner. Stick in thumbtacks at the center of the "X" and the four corners to hold the ribbon in place.

4. Use your ruler to measure about six inches from the two corners on the short sides and eight inches from the corners on the long sides. Stick in a thumbtack to mark the spots where you measured. You should have three tacks on each side. Now cut pieces of ribbon long enough to stretch from thumbtack to thumbtack in a criss-cross pattern (see picture), plus an extra two inches for each ribbon. Lay the ribbons

across the board as shown, then pull out each "marker" thumbtack and use it to hold the ribbon in place at the edge of the board.

5. Turn over the board. Pull the ends of the ribbon around and glue to the back of the board—use tacks to hold them down while glue dries. Then, if you want to, remove all "holder" tacks from the back of the board. Turn the board over and remove all tacks from the edges. For every place where the ribbons cross each other, stick in a tack whose point has been dipped in glue.

6. To hang your bulletin board, use two stick-on fabric-type hangers. (You can find them in a hardware store.) Attach them to either a long side or a short side at about the point where the ribbons are glued.

7. Now it's time to decorate your bulletin board! Use craft glue or a hot glue gun (with adult help) to cover the edges and the thumbtacks with buttons, bows, silk flowers, or paper cutouts. After the glue is dry, your bulletin board is ready to hang and use.

23

Seeing Double

HOW WE SOLVED ALEESHA'S ROOM-SHARING PROBLEM

"Guess what I did after I got home last Saturday?" said Maria. "I painted all my flowerpots! I got the idea from Christine's mom."

"Cool! I want to come over and see!" said Elizabeth. "I have an idea for redecorating, too. I want to do a bulletin board like Christine's, only with horses instead of princess roses."

"That's neat!" said Christine.

About that time, I noticed that Aleesha wasn't saying anything.

"Hey, 'Leesh, when are we going to do your great room makeover?"

"I don't think we can do one for my room, Emilie Marie," she said. "You know, because of my little sister. I was trying to redo my room, like we've been doing, and Marti said it was her room, too, and she liked it the way it was. I just don't think it'll work."

We all sat there for a minute, thinking hard.

I was the first one to break the silence. "I think Marti just wants to be in on the room makeover. So we just need to redecorate a room for two!"

Christine grinned. "So how are we going to do this great room for two makeover?"

Well, first we went over to Aleesha's house and talked to her mom. And then we talked to Marti. We had to think up a good way for Marti's stuff to live with Aleesha's stuff.

I was looking at the wooden bunkbeds where Marti and Aleesha slept. "If you could put curtains on your bed, each of you would have your own private little space."

Marti started jumping up and down. "Like a little playhouse!"

Aleesha clapped her hands. "Neat! I could close the curtains and read in bed at night. But how would we put curtains on the bed?"

"I think you could hang Marti's curtains from the bottom of your bunk...and maybe hang yours from the ceiling," I said.

It took a little while before Aleesha's mom and dad figured out how to hang the curtains. (They did it by fastening plant hanger hooks into the ceiling to hold a curtain rod.) But when they were done, both Aleesha and Marti had their own little private nook.

The next brilliant idea was Christine's—about

how the sisters could organize their stuff. "It's just like this old movie we rented one night—*Yours, Mine, and Ours*! Aleesha's stuff can be one color, and Marti's stuff can be another color. And all the stuff you share can be *both* colors."

"You mean...like this?" asked Aleesha. She pointed to the curtains on their bed, which had yellow and purple and blue and pink flowers. "Maybe I could be purple, like these flowers. And Marti can be yellow, like these flowers."

"Exactly," Christine said, "and all your other stuff can be pink and purple and yellow and blue—kind of multicolored."

Marti and Aleesha both smiled. We could tell they liked the idea for a color-coded room.

On our way out, Aleesha thanked us for all our help. "I know what I'm going to do tonight—close those curtains and *read*!" she said with a big grin.

Aleesha's Fantastic Two-in-a-Room Solutions

Solution One: Color the room "Yours, Mine, and Ours." Pick two go-together colors, one for each of you, and use those colors to show who owns what. Aleesha and Marti used color-coded plastic containers to hold their stuff (purple for Aleesha, yellow for Marti). They also had purple and yellow knobs on their drawers, and they even found purple and yellow hangers for their closet! Then to decorate the stuff that belonged to both of them—the curtains on the windows, the wastebasket, some of the storage containers—they decorated with sheets, wallpaper, and wrapping paper in prints and stripes that used *both* their colors.

Solution Two: Make a private space for each of you. Everyone needs some time to be alone, so think up a way to create an "alone spot" for each of you. Maybe you can set up special "comfy chairs" on different sides of the room with floor pillows, beanbag chairs, and baskets for your stuff.

Solution Three: Make sure each of you has a private place to put your stuff. Everybody needs their own place for special treasures. Marti and Aleesha have two lockable trunks that fit under their bed. Aleesha keeps her diary, her baby ring, and some other stuff in hers. We don't know what Marti keeps in hers!

Solution Four: Don't forget to enjoy the good stuff. Yes, living with your sister can drive you crazy sometimes—but it's also nice to have someone to talk to after the lights go out!

How-To Hints

A Quick and Easy Room Divider

"Milk carton" type crates make a cute and useful room divider. Try to find the stackable kind that fit together closely, and look for them in Yours, Mine, and Ours colors. Line two rows of them facing in opposite directions. Then add another double row on top of the first and maybe even another row. If you want to, use twist-ties or wire to make sure the crates stay together. The rows of crates make great shelves for holding your stuff!

Decorating for Sweet Dreams

You don't just have to decorate your room for daytime. There are a lot of things you can do to make it nice at nighttime, too.

- Buy a package of glow-in-the-dark stars and create a constellation on your ceiling. Or you can make your own stars and planets out of white or yellow posterboard and glow-in-the-dark varnish from a hobby store. Stick them on the ceiling with poster putty, then turn out the lights at night. Awesome!
- Wind strings of white and colored twinkle lights in big plants, on curtain rods, around an iron head-board, or around a window or mirror. You can buy little plastic clips to attach the lights where you want them.
- If you like to read in bed like Aleesha, you can make a book lover's flashlight holder! Find a piece of cardboard tubing that holds the skinny part of your flashlight but doesn't let the bulb part fall through. Punch holes in the end of the tube and put a yarn loop for hanging the holster. Hang it from your headboard or attach it to your wall, and you'll always have a reading light nearby!

Things to Make Your Room Special

A Guardian Angel Nightlight

Since our club is The Angels, I really love this cute Angel nightlight that we made for Aleesha's room. In fact, I liked it so much that I went right home and made one of my own!

newspapers
clear plastic cup (about a 10-ounce size)
strong scissors or craft knife (and adult help)
white tissue paper
water-based decoupage medium (matte finish, from a hobby store) or white glue and water
medium-sized brush (I like the foam kind)
black permanent marker with narrow tip
highlighter pens or watercolor markers
water-based acrylic varnish spray (optional)
plug-in nightlight, about 4" long by 1 1/4" wide
craft glue or hot glue gun (and adult help)

1

1. Spread newspapers to cover your work area. Ask an adult to help you use a craft knife or scissors to cut the cup in half from top to bottom (see diagram 1). One cup will make two nightlights.

2. Trace the angel pattern on p. 27 onto a
2 piece of white tissue paper. Cut it out and tape it to the *inside* of the cup halves so that it shows through. Carefully trace the outline of the angel onto the outside of the cup with the black marker (diagram 2). Remove the pattern. Now cut

or tear more white paper into 1" by 2" pieces.

3. Decoupage medium (or acrylic medium) is a combination glue and sealer. It goes by several names (like Mod Podge or Decoupage Magic) and works great for this project. You can also use plain white glue mixed with a little water. Use the brush to cover the outside of the cup half with decoupage medium. Carefully pick up a piece of tissue paper, lay it on the glue, and gently smooth it down with the brush. Take another piece of tissue paper and lay it on the glue next to the first piece, slightly overlapping. Brush it smooth, too (diagram 3). Keep enough decoupage medium on your brush to glue down all the edges, but not enough to make the paper slide around. Keep adding paper until the whole surface of the plastic is covered, including the bottom of the cup. It's okay to let corners of tissue hang over the edges. Let dry.

4. Now hold the cup up to the light. You should still be able to see the black outline of your angel through the tissue, but you shouldn't see any clear spots. If you do, add another layer of glue and tissue paper and let dry. Trim off any extra paper that hangs off the side.

5. Hold the cup up to the light again and use the marker to trace the angel outline on top of the glued tissue paper. Color your angel with highlighter pens

(so it looks like stained glass) and markers (for colors you can't find in the highlighters). Aleesha's angel has yellow wings and halo, a blue dress, a pretty brown face and hands, and black hair. Use the black marker to make the black outlines a little thicker, to draw in details like the face, and to color in the parts of the cup where the angel isn't— like around the wing tips and halo (diagram 4). Let dry again. If you wish, cover the whole angel with clear acrylic spray to keep the markers from smearing. Then glue the top of the angel (the bottom of the cup) to the top of the nightlight. Your angel should hang over the top like a little lampshade (diagram 5). Now plug in your nightlight and watch your angel shine!

Fifteen-Minute Miracles

How We Learned to Keep Our Rooms Neat *and* Make Them Extra Special

"Well, Emilie Marie," said Christine at our Angels meeting, "what kind of makeover do you want for your room?"

I'd been thinking about that a lot over the past few weeks. But the more I looked around my cozy room, the more I liked it just the way it was—the yellow-striped wallpaper, my collection of teacups, the little table set for tea with my teddy bear guest. I liked the sunshiny windows and the smooth wood floors and the soft rugs.

I just wasn't ready for a big change. "So I guess we're all done with our room makeovers," I said.

"Unless you all want to come back and do my room again!" Elizabeth said.

"Don't tell me it's all messed up already!" said Maria.

"Well, I've been trying to clean it up every Saturday," said Elizabeth. "But I've been busy at your houses, too. Besides, I don't want to spend every weekend cleaning my room."

"Marti and I have been having some problems like that in our room," said Aleesha. "Two people means two times the stuff."

"And I'm always collecting new things," said Maria. "Then I get busy with homework, and it just piles up."

Christine and I looked at each other. I knew we were thinking the same thing. It was something my Grammie taught us.

"I know what you need," I said.

"Me, too," Christine said. And then we both said it together: "Fifteen-minute miracles!"

Aleesha, Elizabeth, and Maria looked at us, confused.

"It really works!" I said. "There's two parts. First...don't put it down..."

"...put it away!" Christine finished. "Like instead of throwing your coat on the bed, you hang it on its hook."

"And instead of putting the book on the floor," I added, "you put it back on the shelf."

"But what about the miracle?" said Maria.

"That's the second

part," I said. "See, most big jobs are lots easier if you do them fifteen minutes at a time. Same with your room—just clean it up fifteen minutes a day. Or even ten minutes. You set a timer, and you work really hard until it rings, and then you stop! And your room stays pretty clean—you can just finish it up fast on Saturday morning."

"I don't think I'd ever get my room clean in fifteen minutes!" said Elizabeth.

"But that's the great part," I said. "Fifteen minutes a day doesn't sound like much—but it's almost two hours a week! So one day you can dust, and another day you can put away your school papers, and another day you can pick up all your toys. It's easy."

"Really?" Elizabeth was still doubtful.

"Well, sometimes I'll have a big craft project to put away, or I'll want to move my stuff around, and that takes more time. But for everyday stuff, fifteen minutes does it."

"What I want to know," said Aleesha, "is what we're going to do *today* if Emilie Marie doesn't want a room makeover?"

"Oh, I have a great idea!" I said. I walked over to a yellow-covered box and pulled out my camera. "I thought we could take some pictures and frame them for our rooms."

And that's just what we did for the rest of that last makeover Saturday. We took a lot of fun pictures of each other in all kinds of poses.

And then came the very best picture of all. My mom came in and took it. And I like it so much that I made a frame for it and had all my friends sign the frame with a paint pen. I have it on my nightstand next to my bed.

It's a picture of me and all my Angel friends standing together in our cleanup aprons. I'm holding a feather duster. Aleesha's cuddling my kitten, Angel, in her arms. Elizabeth is kneeling at the front, holding my teddy. Maria and Christine have their arms around each other. We're all leaning together with silly grins on our faces.

This is what I like best about that picture:

Every morning when I wake up, I look over and see my friends grinning at me. That's a great feeling, because it reminds me of the way we all helped each other and all the fun we had doing our room makeovers. Most of all, it reminds me how lucky I am to have four wonderful friends who care about me.

And that's what makes my room, and my life, really, really special!

Elizabeth's "What I've Learned" Lessons

Elizabeth says, "It might take me awhile, but I've learned a lot about keeping my room neat. Now I have a lot more time on Saturdays to do art projects, read books, and of course play with my best friends!"

Lesson One: Memorize some mottos. Emilie Marie and Christine taught me these little sayings. They're easy to remember, and they really help me keep my room in control! First: *Don't put it down, put it away.* Second: *Don't pile it; file it.* (That one's for your papers.) And finally—my personal favorite: *You can do anything in fifteen minutes a day.* It's really true!

Lesson Two: Break big jobs into little jobs. This is the miracle part of Fifteen-Minute Miracles: Almost any job can be broken down into little jobs and done a little at a time. Don't think, *I need to clean out my entire desk.* Think, *While I'm waiting for Christine's mom to pick me up, I'll clean out this one drawer of my desk.* Then—this is really important— do another drawer the next day!

Lesson Three: Set a timer. The best part of Fifteen-Minute Miracles is that you always know the job will be over soon. I get really speedy when I know that soon the timer will ring and I'll be able to go play!

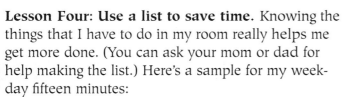

Lesson Four: Use a list to save time. Knowing the things that I have to do in my room really helps me get more done. (You can ask your mom or dad for help making the list.) Here's a sample for my week-day fifteen minutes:
• Make bed
• Quick pick-up—books on shelves, dirty clothes in hamper, papers in filebox
• Clean clothes hung up or put away
• If there's time left, do one weekend chore

And here's what my weekend fifteen minutes might look like:
• Dust
• Clean windows and mirrors and walls
• Sweep, vacuum, or mop

• Take dirty clothes to utility room

Lesson Five: Special projects need a different fifteen minutes. If you want to do a special project in your room, like making an end-of-school scrapbook or putting your pictures in frames, don't use your cleanup minutes. Set a separate time to work on your project—but you can still do it fifteen minutes a day if you want to!

Lesson Six: Work hard—but when you're done, you're done. This is my favorite out of all the lessons I've learned. It's important to keep your room clean and neat and to make it pretty, but it's also important to enjoy fun times with your friends!

How-To Hints
A School-Night Center

If you're like me, it's not super easy to get off to school without losing a library book, forgetting homework, or just getting off to a grumpy start. Here's an idea for making mornings lots nicer by getting things ready the night before.

Start with an old-fashioned hall tree or hat rack if you can find one. (If you can't, you can attach some decorative hooks to the wall.) If you want to, paint the hat rack in colors to match your room. That's where you can hang your clothes for the next day and also your backpack and coat.

Next, place a large wicker laundry basket (or covered box) at the foot of the hall tree. It's for the things you can't hang up—like your library books, cans for the recycling drive, and your shoes and socks. If you want to, you can even add a blackboard or a bulletin board with a checklist of things to

do at night and in the morning.

The idea is that before you go to bed, you get everything ready that you'll need for tomorrow—except maybe your lunch! If you get in the habit of using your school-night center, mornings will go a lot smoother.

You don't have to use a hall tree or hat rack, of course. Any box or bin or hooks will do—if you make sure you use it!

How-To Hints
Emilie Marie's Ready-for-School Checklist

Here's a helpful list of some of the things I usually need to remember before school (both before bed and the next morning). You can copy my checklist and hang it on your wall, or make a list of your own!

Before Bed Checklist
- Homework finished?
- Textbooks to take to school?
- Any papers to be signed or shown to parents?
- Lunch made or lunch money ready?
- Need money for anything at school?
- Any extras to take to school—supplies for projects? book order money?
- Any library books due?
- Clothes laid out?
- Alarm clock set?
- Bath, shower, teeth, etc.?
- Quick room pickup?
- Bedtime prayers?

Before School Checklist
- Make bed?
- Bathroom stuff?
- Get dressed?
- Breakfast?
- Brush teeth?
- Lunch from fridge?
- Backpack and stuff from basket?

Things to Make Your Room Special

A Friend's Gallery

Here is a fun way to display pictures of your family, your friends, and your pets. We made these to display the pictures we took on my room makeover day.

Easy Stand-Up Frame

This cute frame holds a wallet-sized photo (like a friend's school picture) perfectly!

newspapers
piece of 8 1/2" x 11" cardstock, construction paper, or thin cardboard (Cardstock is thicker than notebook paper and thinner than poster board—sort of like an index card. You can get it at an art store or office supply place. Its smooth surface makes a nice frame.)
small piece of posterboard (for the stand)
scissors
craft glue or glue stick
ruler
pencil
picture to frame (I framed a photo that was a little bigger than 2" x 3".)
stickers, paint, or other decorations for trim
thin plastic page protector (from an office store) to make the "glass" in the frame (optional)

1. Protect your work area with newspapers. Then take your cardstock and carefully fold it in half, like a greeting card (see diagram 1). Fold in half again, pressing the folds firmly with your fingers (diagram 2). Hold the folded piece so that it opens like a book and the folded edge is at the bottom. Make a light pencil mark in the center to show where your picture will go (diagram 3).

2. Open the cardstock, which is now divided into four sections. Find the section with the mark and make another mark on the *back* of the same section. Use a ruler and a pencil to draw in the opening for the window around this second mark (diagram 4). Have fun with different shapes—a heart, a circle, a tilted square, etc.

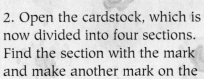

3. To cut out the window, pinch the center of this section with your fingers and snip the pinched part with the scissors. Now you can get your scissors in to cut around the lines.

4. Turn the cardstock over and slip your picture behind the window to see how it fits. Move it around until it looks just right. Then hold the picture in place and turn the frame over. Trace around the outside of the picture. You can also cut out a piece of thin plastic from a page protector to make a "glass" for your frame.

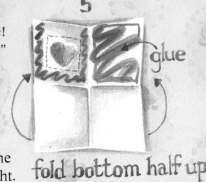

5. Now grab your glue! Make sure the "wrong" side of the cardstock (with the pencil marks) is facing you. First, spread a narrow line of glue around the outside edges of the two sections at the right. Next, carefully spread glue in a "U" shape around the "window" opening. Leave a little space around the picture outline, and don't put any glue above the outline (diagram 5).

6. Fold the bottom half of the picture up to meet the top half. Press firmly, then fold again along the original second fold. Place under a book until glue is dry. Now you have what looks like a book without pages—with the cutout window on the "cover." Glue the "book" together (diagram 6).

7. For the stand, use posterboard and cut a small rectangle. Fold diagonally, as shown (diagram 7). Glue onto back of frame.

8. Now move the folded corner to a position where it holds your frame up. Insert the photo (and "glass") into the front through the unglued top edge. Then use paint pens, markers, stickers, and other things to decorate your frame!